BOARDING KENNELS ARE HOWLIDAY INNS!

THE LINCOLN TUNNEL IS A BIG BORE!

VENUS DE MILO GOT ALL THE BREAKS!

CHILDREN ARE LIVE WHYERS!

MUSTACHES ARE DOWN AT THE MOUTH!

A PICNIC IS A SNACK-IN-THE-GRASS!

THE MARINES DO OFF-SHORE DRILLING!

KING MIDAS HAS A GILT COMPLEX

Roy Doty

DOUBLEDAY & COMPANY, INC.

GARDEN CITY, NEW YORK

Other books in this series

PUNS, GAGS, QUIPS AND RIDDLES
Q'S ARE WEIRD O'S
GUNGA YOUR DIN-DIN IS READY
PINOCCHIO WAS NOSEY

BC 3-0002-60041624-8

Library of Congress Cataloging in Publication Data

Doty, Roy, 1922–
    King Midas has a gilt complex.

    SUMMARY: An illustrated collection of jokes,
riddles, puns, and gags.
    1. Riddles—Juvenile literature.   [1. Riddles.
2. Joke books] I. Title.
PN6371.5.D576   818'.5'407

ISBN 0-385-13488-6 Trade
    0-385-13489-4 Prebound
Library of Congress Catalog Card Number 77-19226

ROY DOTY is a nationally known free-lance artist whose work regularly appears in numerous major publications such as *Newsweek, Business Week,* and the New York *Times.* He is familiar to *Popular Science* readers as author-cartoonist of the monthly "Wordless Workshop," and his "Laugh-In" newspaper comic strip was nationally syndicated. An inventor and do-it-yourself hobbyist, Mr. Doty is the creator of the Popular Science Picture Clock Kit. He lives in Connecticut with his authoress wife and four children.

BO-PEEP HANGS AROUND WITH CROOKS!

DISC JOCKEYS ARE RADIO-ACTIVE!

BARBED WIRE IS A RIP-OFF!

MAVERICKS ARE BUM STEERS!

BROWN SUGAR IS AMBER DEXTROSE

SPANKING IS STERN PUNISHMENT!

JOGGING IS ALL-IN FUN!

NAILS ARE DRIVE-INS!

KING KONG WAS BORN LITTLE AND GREW SOME!

YOGURT IS VERY CULTURED!

GIVE YOUR BATHTUB A RING!